Poems of
John Milton

Poems of
John Milton

*Selected and with an Introduction
by* CLAIRE TOMALIN

PENGUIN CLASSICS
an imprint of
PENGUIN BOOKS

PENGUIN CLASSICS

Published by the Penguin Group
Penguin Books Ltd, 80 Strand, London WC2R ORL, England
Penguin Group (USA) Inc., 375 Hudson Street, New York, New York 10014, USA
Penguin Group (Canada), 90 Eglinton Avenue East, Suite 700, Toronto, Ontario,
Canada M4P 2Y3 (a division of Pearson Penguin Canada Inc.)
Penguin Ireland, 25 St Stephen's Green, Dublin 2, Ireland (a division of Penguin Books Ltd)
Penguin Group (Australia), 250 Camberwell Road, Camberwell, Victoria 3124, Australia
(a division of Pearson Australia Group Pty Ltd)
Penguin Books India Pvt Ltd, 11 Community Centre,
Panchsheel Park, New Delhi – 110 017, India
Penguin Group (NZ), 67 Apollo Drive, Rosedale, North Shore 0632, New Zealand
(a division of Pearson New Zealand Ltd)
Penguin Books (South Africa) (Pty) Ltd, 24 Sturdee Avenue,
Rosebank, Johannesburg 2196, South Africa

Penguin Books Ltd, Registered Offices: 80 Strand, London WC2R ORL, England

www.penguin.com

This selection first published 2008

1

Selection and Introduction copyright © Claire Tomalin, 2008

The moral right of the editor has been asserted

Set in 10/12.5pt PostScript Adobe Sabon
Typeset by Rowland Phototypesetting Ltd, Bury St Edmunds, Suffolk
Printed in England by Clays Ltd, St Ives plc

A CIP catalogue record for this book is available from the British Library

ISBN: 978-1-846-14033-4

www.greenpenguin.co.uk

Mixed Sources
Product group from well-managed
forests and other controlled sources
www.fsc.org Cert no. SA-COC-1592
© 1996 Forest Stewardship Council

Penguin Books is committed to a sustainable future
for our business, our readers and our planet.
The book in your hands is made from paper
certified by the Forest Stewardship Council.

Contents

The Sonnets

The Last Years

Introduction

John Milton was a Londoner. He lived through the most stirring years in English history, and gave his life to poetry and to politics. He was born in 1608 in Bread Street, near Cheapside, while Shakespeare was still writing, and died in Artillery Walk (now Bunhill Row) in 1674. Little is known of his mother, but his father was a prosperous man, a dealer in property and finance who also composed and published music. This meant that the boy learnt about rhythm and melody early; he sang and played the organ and the bass viol. Outstandingly gifted in his other studies, he was also a hard worker. His father intended him for the Church, but he made up his mind young to become a poet. He had a facility for languages, mastering Latin, Greek, Hebrew, French and Italian, and as a schoolboy wrote verses in Latin and Greek, and continued to write in Latin and in Italian.

He was first taught by private tutors and then sent to St Paul's School. In 1625, the year that brought Charles I to the throne, he went up to Christ's College, Cambridge, where his fellow students nicknamed him 'the Lady of Christ's', mocking his girlish looks and also perhaps his piety and chastity. An unladylike quarrel with his tutor led to his being rusticated for a term, but during his Cambridge years he began to make a reputation as a poet among his friends and contemporaries. After graduating he returned home to his parents and devoted himself to further study and to poetry. The family moved out of the City, first to Hammersmith and then to Horton, now in Berkshire but then in Buckinghamshire. His first published poem, 'On Shakespeare. 1630', was printed in the Second Folio of 1632, anonymously, alongside other tributes. He was writing odes and sonnets, and in 1634 his first major work, a masque, was acted, and published three years later, again anonymously. It is known as *Comus*, the name of the magician who tries to ensnare a virtuous young woman with the pleasures of the senses, only to have her talk him down. The conflict was one Milton understood well, as a puritan who responded keenly to the delights offered by the natural world: spring sunshine, flowers, fruits, music, love and the beauty of women, to which he devoted some of his early Latin verses (e.g., 'Elegy VII') and three Italian sonnets.

'L'Allegro' and 'Il Penseroso' are also from the early 1630s, twin celebrations of the contrasting joys of merriment and gloom, and of the English landscape, and crammed with literary allusions. They have always been admired, so that even those who don't know the source are likely to recognize lines from them. Purcell set them to music, and Dr Johnson, although he had harsh things to say of much of Milton's poetry – which he accused of artificiality and lack of human interest – announced that 'every man that reads them, reads them with pleasure.'

Then, in November 1637, came 'Lycidas', an elegy to a college friend, Edward King, drowned at sea. Milton adopted the pastoral convention of antiquity and presented himself as a shepherd mourning for another, invoking nymphs, satyrs, fauns, classical sites and gods. Out of this deliberately artificial mode and its musical, echoing, repetitive phrasing, the poem leaps into life with

some powerful images. One is of the drowned body of
his friend:

> . . . whilst thee the shores, and sounding seas
> Wash far away, where'er thy bones are hurled,
> Whether beyond the stormy Hebrides,
> Where thou perhaps under the whelming tide
> Visit'st the bottom of the monstrous world . . .

It has been suggested that 'Lycidas' presents Milton's
decision to turn aside from the inner life and vocation
of poet to the external world of travel, politics and matri-
mony. To represent this change of direction the shepherd
who speaks the elegy is shown in the last lines leaving his
subject behind as he departs for 'fresh fields and pastures
new'. And in fact, after completing 'Lycidas', Milton
did set off for the Continent, travelling for over a year
through France and Italy, and when he arrived back in
1639 he established his own household, took in pupils
and within three years found a wife.

After 'Lycidas' there was no more English poetry for
over twenty years, except for a dozen or so sonnets – but
the exception is an important one. His subjects were
chosen eclectically, even eccentrically, with themes vary-
ing from a comic complaint about the reception of a
prose pamphlet he had written to a resounding protest
against a Catholic-inspired massacre in the Alps; from
a meditation on the pleasure of sharing food, wine and
music with a friend to an account of inmost loss and
sorrow in the last and most perfect of his sonnets. His
choreographic skill with words, and the force behind
each idea and feeling, combine to make these master
works.

Just before the outbreak of the Civil War in the

summer of 1642, Milton made an impulsive choice of a bride, a young woman half his age, Mary Powell. After six weeks as his wife she chose to go home to her parents in the country and refused to return: she was young, she missed her family, and her husband failed to delight her. He was left bitter and aggrieved at having his expectations of married life so quickly dashed, even though, like most men of his time, he did not think of women as intellectual companions. Yet in *Paradise Lost* he makes Adam value the friendship in marriage above sexual passion, a piece of wisdom Milton may have acquired ruefully from his own hasty choice of a bride.

He now devoted himself to the great questions of the day: how the conflict between King and Parliament should be resolved, how a country should be governed – whether by King or Parliament or Protector – and whether it should have lords and bishops and an established Church. He produced pamphlets on these and other subjects such as education and, notably, his great defence of the freedom of the press, *Areopagitica*, in 1644. Prompted by his own marital situation, he also wrote advocating divorce as a solution to unhappy marriages, and thought of finding another wife.

As the war continued his eyesight, never good, and taxed by long hours of reading in dim light, deteriorated. His wife, after three years' absence, begged his pardon and returned to him. Over the next years she bore him three daughters and a short-lived son. They moved house, first to Barbican and then High Holborn, backing on to Lincoln's Inn Fields. In January 1646 a collection of his early poems was published (dated 1645). After the execution of the King in 1649 he accepted an appointment as Secretary for Foreign Tongues (effectively Latin Secretary) to the Council of State, dealing with Cromwell's correspondence with foreign governments. He was given lodgings in Scotland Yard, then took a house in Petty-France, opening into St James's Park. His eyes got worse under the strain of his official work, and by 1652 he was blind. In the same year Mary died in childbirth, leaving him with three small daughters. He did not think it worth educating girls, and they had an unhappy home and grew up disliking their father. He married again in 1656, only to lose his second, much loved wife Katherine Woodcock after fifteen months, her child also dying.

During the months before the restoration of Charles II Milton published pamphlets in favour of a republican form of government, and when the King arrived in England in May 1660 Milton went into hiding. Some of his books were publicly burned and he was imprisoned for a short time in the Tower, and fined. The poet Andrew Marvell protested in Parliament about the fine, and Milton escaped a death penalty. His disgrace was not surprising, given that he had opposed the royalist cause, worked for Cromwell's administration and publicly defended the execution of the King. In these sombre circumstances, and knowing that his religious and political creeds had failed, Milton produced the epic *Paradise Lost*, long planned, begun in 1658, composed in his head and dictated to assistants. His third marriage was arranged through friends in 1663, his new wife, Elizabeth, being thirty years his junior, and she kept him comfortable during his last years.

Paradise Lost was probably completed in 1663, but the first report of a reading comes from Milton's Quaker friend Thomas Ellwood in 1665. This was the year of the Great Plague, and Ellwood helped Milton to escape it by renting a house for him in Chalfont St Giles in

Buckinghamshire (the only one of his dwellings still standing). The poem was published quietly in 1667. Milton was paid £5 by the printer, the first edition was of 1,300 copies, and he was promised another £5 if a second edition should be called for. A few readers immediately saw its importance. Milton made revisions for the second edition, and the young Dryden dramatized it. *Paradise Regained* and *Samson Agonistes*, a verse drama modelled on the Greek tragedies, were published in 1671, and in 1673 an enlarged collection of his short poems. Milton died in 1674, aged sixty-five, and was buried by the altar in St Giles, Cripplegate, which was bombed in the Second World War and is now within the Barbican site. In 1688, the year James II was overthrown, to be replaced by William III, a fine fourth edition of *Paradise Lost* was published and sold by subscription, and, with this and the change of political climate, Milton's reputation as a great poet was established. In 1737 a monument was put up to him in Westminster Abbey.

What makes Milton difficult also makes him fascinating. It is the way he uses in his poetry every story, every landscape, every mythical creature and god of Greece and Rome he has read about, every allusion from Shakespeare, Spenser, Ovid, Horace or Chaucer that has taken his fancy, cramming them in not simply to beautify but because this is how he experiences the world, as a huge, continuous panorama of the imagination, knowledge and perceptions of earlier writers. To read him you need some understanding of who Alcestis, Ceres, Hebe, Hermes, Latona or Electra (and so on) were. This is why I have included explanatory notes. Once you can follow the allusions, the poems open up.

The beauty of the poetry is achieved through formality, its effects studied, with nothing of Keats's 'fine excess' or Shakespeare's or Donne's new-minted metaphors; but so perfectly studied that it compels constant surprise and admiration for the grandeur and variety of the sentence structure, the musicality of the lines, the energy and subtlety of his use of words. Hazlitt wrote that 'the fervour of his imagination melts down and renders malleable, as in a furnace, the most contradictory materials.' No other Christian writer has drawn so insistently and lovingly on the myths of the Greeks and Romans, so that in his description of the Garden of Eden, where God placed Adam and Eve, he compares it with

> ... that fair field
> Of Enna, where Prosérpine gath'ring flow'rs
> Herself a fairer flow'r by gloomy Dis
> Was gathered, which cost Ceres all that pain
> To seek her through the world ...

It is an astonishing leap out of a Christian world picture and into a pagan, here taken from Ovid, who describes how Proserpina, daughter of Ceres, the goddess of harvests, is carried off by Dis, the god of the underworld, from Enna in Sicily, and how Ceres searches for her and, failing to find her, consigns the world to perpetual winter until her daughter is restored to her; and the leap is accepted unhesitatingly by the reader, who also understands that Proserpina is seen as a version of Eve, another vulnerable and beautiful creature attacked by a hellish predator.

Paradise Lost is full of these juxtapositions as it narrates the Christian story of the rebellious angels, the making of Hell, the creation of Adam and Eve, their love and enjoyment of the garden in which God places them, Eve's temptation by Satan and their fall. Even in the last lines of the poem, as they are expelled from Paradise, the severe Protestant Milton gives way to the Milton who had absorbed a classical, humanist picture, and he shows them asserting their human resolve and comradeship, less like humiliated sinners than chastened yet proud, intelligent and courageous spirits:

> Some natural tears they dropped, but wiped them soon;
> The world was all before them, where to choose
> Their place of rest, and Providence their guide:
> They hand in hand with wand'ring steps and slow,
> Through Eden took their solitary way.

The directness and plainness of Milton's language here, mostly monosyllabic, without imagery or ornament, bring his story to a flawless and unforgettable conclusion.

Milton's reputation as one of the great English poets, well established by the eighteenth century in spite of Johnson's cavils, was reaffirmed by the Romantics – Blake illustrated his work, and Wordsworth exclaimed, 'Milton! thou should'st be living at this hour' – and by later nineteenth-century critics. Macaulay wrote fine essays about him, and David Masson produced a seven-volume *Life of Milton* between 1859 and 1894, which, although overtaken in points of scholarship by later biographies, is still a magnificent monument. It took the twentieth century and T. S. Eliot, followed by F. R. Leavis, both influential critics, to launch a demolition job on Milton's poetry, accusing him of writing English as if it were a dead language. The most brilliant refutation came from Christopher Ricks in his *Milton's Grand Style*

(1963). This selection avails itself of John Leonard's excellent one-volume *John Milton: The Complete Poems* (Penguin Classics, 1998). Interested readers might want to look at John Carey's superb edition of *The Complete Shorter Poems* and Alastair Fowler's of *Paradise Lost*, both available in paperback.

The Schoolboy

Some verses from Milton's metrical version of Psalm CXXXVI

This was made in 1624, when he was fifteen. Hymn singers will know its listing of God's blessings well, the 'golden-tressèd sun' and 'hornèd moon ... Amongst her spangled sisters bright'. He published it in his first collection in 1645.

> Let us with a gladsome mind
> Praise the Lord, for he is kind.
>> For his mercies ay endure,
>> Ever faithful, ever sure.

> Let us blaze his name abroad,
> For of gods he is the God;
>> For, &c.

> O let us his praises tell,
> That doth the wrathful tyrants quell.
>> For, &c.

> That with his miracles doth make
> Amazèd heav'n and earth to shake.
>> For, &c.

> That by his wisdom did create
> The painted heav'ns so full of state.
>> For, &c.

> That did the solid earth ordain
> To rise above the wat'ry plain.
>> For, &c.

That by his all-commanding might,
Did fill the new-made world with light.
   For, &c.

And caused the golden-tressèd sun,
All the day long his course to run.
   For, &c.

The hornèd moon to shine by night,
Amongst her spangled sisters bright.
   For, &c.

. . .

All living creatures he doth feed,
And with full hand supplies their need.
   For, &c.

Let us therefore warble forth
His mighty majesty and worth.
   For, &c.

That his mansion hath on high
Above the reach of mortal eye.
   For his mercies ay endure,
   Ever faithful, ever sure.

The University Wit

Lines *from* At a Vacation Exercise
in the College

This was read by Milton to his fellow students at Christ's College, Cambridge, in July 1628, as part of an entertainment made up of Latin prose and English verse. Milton published the English part in his collection of 1673. These are the opening lines:

Hail native language, that by sinews weak
Didst move my first endeavouring tongue to speak,
And mad'st imperfect words with childish trips,
Half unpronounced, slide through my infant lips,
Driving dumb silence from the portal door,
Where he had mutely sat two years before:
Here I salute thee and thy pardon ask,
That now I use thee in my latter task:
Small loss it is that thence can come unto thee,
I know my tongue but little grace can do thee.
Thou need'st not be ambitious to be first,
Believe me I have thither packed the worst:
And, if it happen as I did forecast,
The daintiest dishes shall be served up last.
I pray thee then deny me not thy aid
For this same small neglect that I have made:
But haste thee straight to do me once a pleasure,
And from thy wardrobe bring thy chiefest treasure;
Not those new-fangled toys, and trimming slight
Which takes our late fantastics with delight,
But cull those richest robes, and gay'st attire
Which deepest spirits, and choicest wits desire:
I have some naked thoughts that rove about
And loudly knock to have their passage out;

And weary of their place do only stay
Till thou hast decked them in thy best array;
That so they may without suspect or fears
Fly swiftly to this fair assembly's ears . . .

Song. On May Morning

Ten lines welcoming the spring, written about 1629, and so probably during the Easter Term at Cambridge. First published 1645.

Now the bright morning star, day's harbinger,
Comes dancing from the east, and leads with her
The flowery May, who from her green lap throws
The yellow cowslip, and the pale primrose.
   Hail bounteous May that dost inspire
   Mirth and youth, and warm desire;
   Woods and groves are of thy dressing,
   Hill and dale doth boast thy blessing.
Thus we salute thee with our early song,
And welcome thee, and wish thee long.

Lines from On the Morning of
Christ's Nativity

Milton told the great friend of his youth, Charles Diodati, that he started writing this poem before dawn on Christmas Day 1629, when he would have been at home for the vacation. This was shortly after his twenty-first birthday. He published it in his 1645 collection.

No war, or battle's sound
Was heard the world around:
   The idle spear and shield were high up hung;
The hookèd chariot stood
Unstained with hostile blood,
   The trumpet spake not to the armèd throng,
And kings sat still with awful eye,
As if they surely knew their sov'reign Lord was by.

But peaceful was the night
Wherein the Prince of Light
   His reign of peace upon the earth began:
The winds with wonder whist,
Smoothly the waters kissed,
   Whispering new joys to the mild Oceán,
Who now hath quite forgot to rave,
While birds of calm sit brooding on the charmèd wave.

The stars with deep amaze
Stand fixed in steadfast gaze,
    Bending one way their precious influence,
And will not take their flight,
For all the morning light,
    Or Lucifer[1] that often warned them thence;
But in their glimmering orbs did glow,
Until their Lord himself bespake, and bid them go.

And though the shady gloom
Had given day her room,
    The sun himself withheld his wonted speed,
And hid his head for shame,
As his inferior flame,
    The new-enlightened world no more should need;
He saw a greater Sun appear
Than his bright throne, or burning axle-tree could bear.

The shepherds on the lawn,
Or ere the point of dawn,
    Sat simply chatting in a rustic row;
Full little thought they then,
That the mighty Pan[2]
    Was kindly come to live with them below;
Perhaps their loves, or else their sheep,
Was all that did their silly thoughts so busy keep.

1. Lucifer is the morning star, now known to be the same as Venus.
2. Pan, the Greek god of shepherds, was sometimes identified with Christ.

On Shakespeare. 1630

Milton himself dated this 1630 in the 1645 edition of his poems. It was first printed anonymously, among prefatory material to the Shakespeare Second Folio. Milton was seven when Shakespeare died. He revered his work, and his own early poems especially are rich in Shakespearean echoes.

What needs my Shakespeare for his honoured bones,
The labour of an age in pilèd stones,
Or that his hallowed relics should be hid
Under a star-ypointing pyramid?
Dear son of Memory, great heir of fame,
What need'st thou such weak witness of thy name?
Thou in our wonder and astonishment
Hast built thyself a live-long monument.
For whilst to th' shame of slow-endeavouring art,
Thy easy numbers flow, and that each heart
Hath from the leaves of thy unvalued[1] book,
Those Delphic lines[2] with deep impression took,
Then thou, our fancy of itself bereaving,
Dost make us marble with too much conceiving;
And so sepúlchred in such pomp dost lie,
That kings for such a tomb would wish to die.

1. 'unvalued' here means 'invaluable'.
2. 'Delphic lines' are inspired by Apollo, the god of poetry, whose temple was at Delphi on the slopes of Mount Parnassus, where he supposedly lived with the Muses.

On the University Carrier

Who sickened in the time of his vacancy, being forbid
to go to London, by reason of the plague

Hobson, the 86-year-old driver of the chief transport
between Cambridge and the Bull Inn in Bishopsgate,
London, was known to everyone in the university, and
his death on 1 January 1631 inspired many poems. This
is the first of two by Milton. His joke – that Hobson was
caught by Death only because he had to stop working
because there was plague in London – may well have
been the truth of the matter. First published in the 1645
collection.

Here lies old Hobson, Death hath broke his girt,[1]
And here alas, hath laid him in the dirt,
Or else the ways being foul, twenty to one,
He's here stuck in a slough, and overthrown.
'Twas such a shifter, that if truth were known,
Death was half glad when he had got him down;
For he had any time these ten years full,
Dodged with him, betwixt Cambridge and the Bull.
And surely, Death could never have prevailed,
Had not his weekly course of carriage failed;
But lately finding him so long at home,
And thinking how his journey's end was come,
And that he had ta'en up his latest inn,
In the kind office of a chamberlain

---

1. 'girt' is a saddle belt.

Showed him his room where he must lodge that night,
Pulled off his boots, and took away the light:
If any ask for him, it shall be said,
Hobson has supped, and 's newly gone to bed.

L'Allegro *and* Il Penseroso

The poems are a pair, each starting with a grand operatic flourish before moving into neat, agile couplets that set out the charms of imaginary yet recognizably English scenes and landscapes. The first celebrates cheerfulness, the second melancholy. Their date of composition is uncertain, but they were probably written between 1629 and 1632, while Milton was still based in Cambridge. They were first published in 1645.

L'Allegro

Hence loathèd Melancholy,
    Of Cerberus,[1] and blackest Midnight born,
In Stygian cave forlorn,
    'Mongst horrid shapes, and shrieks, and sights unholy,
Find out some uncouth cell,
    Where brooding Darkness spreads his jealous wings,
And the night-raven sings;
    There under ebon shades, and low-browed rocks,
As ragged as thy locks,
    In dark Cimmerian desert ever dwell.[2]
But come thou goddess fair and free,
In Heav'n yclept Euphrosyne,[3]

---

1. Cerberus was the many-headed dog who guarded the entrance to the underworld, close to the River Styx.
2. The Cimmerian Desert represents the edge of the world.

3. Euphrosyne's sisters were Aglaia and Thalia, representing Brightness and Bloom respectively, here given two possible sets of parents: Venus, the goddess of love, and Bacchus, the god of wine; or Aurora, the

And by men, heart-easing Mirth,
Whom lovely Venus at a birth
With two sister Graces more
To ivy-crownèd Bacchus bore;
Or whether (as some sager sing)
The frolic wind that breathes the spring,
Zephyr with Aurora playing,
As he met her once a-Maying,
There on beds of violets blue,
And fresh-blown roses washed in dew,
Filled her with thee a daughter fair,
So buxom, blithe, and debonair.
Haste thee nymph, and bring with thee
Jest and youthful Jollity,
Quips and Cranks, and wanton Wiles,
Nods, and Becks, and wreathèd Smiles,
Such as hang on Hebe's cheek,[4]
And love to live in dimple sleek;
Sport that wrinkled Care derides,
And Laughter holding both his sides.
Come, and trip it as ye go
On the light fantastic toe,
And in thy right hand lead with thee,
The mountain nymph, sweet Liberty;[5]
And if I give thee honour due,
Mirth, admit me of thy crew
To live with her, and live with thee,
In unreprovèd pleasures free;

---

goddess of dawn, and Zephyr, the
personification of the west wind
(also known as Favonius).
4. Hebe was the goddess of youth
and cup-bearer to the gods.
5. The mountain nymphs were
known as Oreads (or Oreades),
from *oros*, 'mountain', and were
the companions of Diana, the
celibate goddess of the hunt, which
may be why Milton associated
them with liberty.

To hear the lark begin his flight,
And singing startle the dull night,
From his watch-tower in the skies,
Till the dappled dawn doth rise;
Then to come in spite of sorrow,
And at my window bid good morrow,
Through the sweet-briar, or the vine,
Or the twisted eglantine.
While the cock with lively din,
Scatters the rear of darkness thin,
And to the stack, or the barn door,
Stoutly struts his dames before,
Oft list'ning how the hounds and horn,
Cheerly rouse the slumb'ring morn,
From the side of some hoar hill,
Through the high wood echoing shrill.
Some time walking not unseen
By hedge-row elms, on hillocks green,
Right against the eastern gate,
Where the great sun begins his state,
Robed in flames, and amber light,
The clouds in thousand liveries dight.
While the ploughman near at hand,
Whistles o'er the furrowed land,
And the milkmaid singeth blithe,
And the mower whets his scythe,
And every shepherd tells his tale
Under the hawthorn in the dale.
Straight mine eye hath caught new pleasures
Whilst the landscape round it measures,
Russet lawns, and fallows grey,
Where the nibbling flocks do stray,
Mountains on whose barren breast
The labouring clouds do often rest:

Meadows trim with daisies pied,
Shallow brooks, and rivers wide.
Towers, and battlements it sees
Bosomed high in tufted trees,
Where perhaps some beauty lies,
The Cynosure[6] of neighbouring eyes.
Hard by, a cottage chimney smokes,
From betwixt two agèd oaks,
Where Corydon[7] and Thyrsis met,
Are at their savoury dinner set
Of herbs, and other country messes,
Which the neat-handed Phyllis dresses;
And then in haste her bower she leaves,
With Thestylis to bind the sheaves;
Or if the earlier season lead
To the tanned haycock in the mead,
Sometimes with secure delight
The upland hamlets will invite,
When the merry bells ring round,
And the jocund rebecks[8] sound
To many a youth, and many a maid,
Dancing in the chequered shade;
And young and old come forth to play
On a sunshine holiday,
Till the livelong daylight fail,
Then to the spicy nut-brown ale,
With stories told of many a feat,
How faery Mab[9] the junkets ate;

6. 'Cynosure' is the Pole Star, hence the pre-eminent local beauty.
7. Corydon, Thyrsis, Phyllis and Thestylis were standard names for shepherds and country girls in classical writers such as Virgil.

8. A 'rebeck' is a three-stringed medieval violin.
9. Faery Mab was an established figure in popular English mythology – see, for example, Mercutio's speech in *Romeo and*

She was pinched, and pulled she said,
And he by friar's lantern led,
Tells how the drudging goblin sweat,
To earn his cream-bowl duly set,
When in one night, ere glimpse of morn,
His shadowy flail hath threshed the corn
That ten day-labourers could not end,
Then lies him down the lubber fiend,
And stretched out all the chimney's length,
Basks at the fire his hairy strength;
And crop-full out of doors he flings,
Ere the first cock his matin rings.
Thus done the tales, to bed they creep,
By whispering winds soon lulled asleep.
Towered cities please us then,
And the busy hum of men,
Where throngs of knights and barons bold,
In weeds of peace high triumphs hold,
With store of ladies, whose bright eyes
Rain influence, and judge the prize
Of wit, or arms, while both contend
To win her grace, whom all commend.
There let Hymen[10] oft appear
In saffron robe, with taper clear,
And pomp, and feast, and revelry,
With masque and antique pageantry;
Such sights as youthful poets dream
On summer eves by haunted stream.

Juliet. The 'friar' with his lantern is the Will o' the Wisp, and the 'drudging goblin' is Robin Goodfellow, or Puck.

10. Hymen was the Greek god of marriage, always shown crowned with flowers and carrying a flaming torch.

Then to the well-trod stage anon,
If Jonson's learned sock[11] be on,
Or sweetest Shakespeare, Fancy's child,
Warble his native wood-notes wild.
And ever against eating cares,
Lap me in soft Lydian airs,[12]
Married to immortal verse
Such as the meeting soul may pierce
In notes, with many a winding bout
Of linkèd sweetness long drawn out,
With wanton heed, and giddy cunning,
The melting voice through mazes running;
Untwisting all the chains that tie
The hidden soul of harmony.
That Orpheus'[13] self may heave his head
From golden slumber on a bed
Of heaped Elysian flow'rs, and hear
Such strains as would have won the ear
Of Pluto, to have quite set free
His half-regained Eurydice.
These delights, if thou canst give,
Mirth with thee, I mean to live.

11. The 'sock' was a slipper worn by comic actors in Antiquity, Ben Jonson, a modern master of comedy.
12. 'Lydian airs' were gentle, as opposed to martial music.
13. When Eurydice, the wife of the minstrel Orpheus, died of a snake bite, he went into the underworld to try to bring her back. Pluto, the god who ruled the underworld, said he could take her if he did not look back at her as she followed him, but Orpheus could not resist turning to see her, and so lost her irrevocably.

Il Penseroso

Hence vain deluding joys,
  The brood of Folly without father bred,
How little you bestead,
  Or fill the fixèd mind with all your toys;
Dwell in some idle brain,
  And fancies fond with gaudy shapes possess,
As thick and numberless
  As the gay motes that people the sunbeams,
Or likest hovering dreams,
  The fickle pensioners of Morpheus'[1] train.
But hail thou goddess, sage and holy,
Hail divinest Melancholy,
Whose saintly visage is too bright
To hit the sense of human sight;
And therefore to our weaker view,
O'erlaid with black staid Wisdom's hue.
Black, but such as in esteem,
Prince Memnon's[2] sister might beseem,
Or that starred Ethiop queen that strove
To set her beauty's praise above
The sea-nymphs, and their powers offended;
Yet thou art higher far descended,
Thee bright-haired Vesta[3] long of yore,
To solitary Saturn bore;

1. Morpheus was the god of dreams or sleep, usually shown as a fat, winged, dozing child.
2. Memnon, a king of Ethiopia, went to Troy to support his uncle Priam and was killed there; the Ethiop queen was Cassiopeia, turned into a constellation after boasting that she was more beautiful than the Nereids.
3. Vesta was the Roman goddess of hearth and home. Milton makes her a daughter of Saturn, who ruled before Jove, and mother of Cassiopeia, although Vesta is traditionally a virgin.

His daughter she (in Saturn's reign,
Such mixture was not held a stain).
Oft in glimmering bow'rs and glades
He met her, and in secret shades
Of woody Ida's inmost grove,
While yet there was no fear of Jove.
Come pensive nun, devout and pure,
Sober, steadfast, and demure,
All in a robe of darkest grain,
Flowing with majestic train,
And sable stole of cypress lawn,[4]
Over thy decent shoulders drawn.
Come, but keep thy wonted state,
With even step, and musing gait,
And looks commercing with the skies,
Thy rapt soul sitting in thine eyes:
There held in holy passion still,
Forget thyself to marble, till
With a sad leaden downward cast,
Thou fix them on the earth as fast.
And join with thee calm Peace, and Quiet,
Spare Fast, that oft with gods doth diet,
And hears the Muses in a ring,
Ay round about Jove's altar sing.
And add to these retired Leisure,
That in trim gardens takes his pleasure;
But first, and chiefest, with thee bring,
Him that yon soars on golden wing,
Guiding the fiery-wheelèd throne,
The Cherub Contemplatïon,
And the mute Silence hist along,
'Less Philomel[5] will deign a song,

4. Cypress lawn is a fine black fabric.

5. Philomel is the nightingale, Cynthia the moon.

In her sweetest, saddest plight,
Smoothing the rugged brow of Night,
While Cynthia checks her dragon yoke,
Gently o'er th' accustomed oak;
Sweet bird that shunn'st the noise of folly,
Most musical, most melancholy!
Thee chantress oft the woods among,
I woo to hear thy even-song;
And missing thee, I walk unseen
On the dry smooth-shaven green,
To behold the wand'ring moon,
Riding near her highest noon,
Like one that had been led astray
Through the heav'n's wide pathless way;
And oft, as if her head she bowed,
Stooping through a fleecy cloud.
Oft on a plat of rising ground,
I hear the far-off curfew sound,
Over some wide-watered shore,
Swinging slow with sullen roar;
Or if the air will not permit,
Some still removèd place will fit,
Where glowing embers through the room
Teach light to counterfeit a gloom,
Far from all resort of mirth,
Save the cricket on the hearth,
Or the bellman's drowsy charm,
To bless the doors from nightly harm:
Or let my lamp at midnight hour,
Be seen in some high lonely tow'r,
Where I may oft outwatch the Bear,[6]
With thrice-great Hermes, or unsphere

6. The constellation of the Bear
never sets, so to outwatch it is to sit
up all night. The god, 'thrice-great
Hermes', is here associated with the

The spirit of Plato to unfold
What worlds, or what vast regions hold
The immortal mind that hath forsook
Her mansion in this fleshly nook:
And of those daemons that are found
In fire, air, flood, or under ground,
Whose power hath a true consent
With planet, or with element.
Sometime let gorgeous Tragedy
In sceptred pall come sweeping by,
Presenting Thebes,[7] or Pelops' line,
Or the tale of Troy divine.
Or what (though rare) of later age,
Ennobled hath the buskined stage.
But, O sad virgin, that thy power
Might raise Musaeus[8] from his bower,
Or bid the soul of Orpheus sing
Such notes as warbled to the string,
Drew iron tears down Pluto's cheek,
And made Hell grant what love did seek.
Or call up him that left half-told
The story of Cambuscan[9] bold,
Of Camball, and of Algarsife,
And who had Canace to wife,

Hermetic books of the Neo-Platonic philosophers, which dealt with philosophy, alchemy and magic.
7. Oedipus, King of Thebes, was the hero of tragedies by Sophocles. Pelops was the father of Atreus and grandfather of Agamemnon, whose family was the subject of plays by all three of the greatest Greek playwrights, Aeschylus, Sophocles and Euripides.

8. Musaeus was a pupil of Orpheus. For Orpheus, see last note to 'L'Allegro'.
9. Cambuscan is Chaucer's version of the name of Genghis Khan, 'the Tartar king', the subject of his unfinished Squire's Tale, completed by Spenser. His sons were Camball and Algarsife, his daughter Canace.

That owned the virtuous ring and glass,
And of the wondrous horse of brass,
On which the Tartar king did ride;
And if aught else, great bards beside,
In sage and solemn tunes have sung,
Of tourneys and of trophies hung;
Of forests, and enchantments drear,
Where more is meant than meets the ear.
Thus Night oft see me in thy pale career,
Till civil-suited Morn appear,
Not tricked and frounced as she was wont,
With the Attic boy[10] to hunt,
But kerchiefed in a comely cloud,
While rocking winds are piping loud,
Or ushered with a shower still,
When the gust hath blown his fill,
Ending on the rustling leaves,
With minute drops from off the eaves.
And when the sun begins to fling
His flaring beams, me goddess bring
To archèd walks of twilight groves,
And shadows brown that Sylvan[11] loves
Of pine, or monumental oak,
Where the rude axe with heavèd stroke,
Was never heard the nymphs to daunt,
Or fright them from their hallowed haunt.
There in close covert by some brook,
Where no profaner eye may look,
Hide me from Day's garish eye,
While the bee with honeyed thigh,

10. The 'Attic boy' here is
Cephalus, a hunter, beloved of
Aurora (Dawn).

11. Sylvan or Sylvanus was the god
of fields and forests.

That at her flow'ry work doth sing,
And the waters murmuring
With such consort as they keep,
Entice the dewy-feathered Sleep;
And let some strange mysterious dream,
Wave at his wings in airy stream,
Of lively portraiture displayed,
Softly on my eyelids laid.
And as I wake, sweet music breathe
Above, about, or underneath,
Sent by some spirit to mortals good,
Or th' unseen Genius of the wood.
But let my due feet never fail,
To walk the studious cloister's pale,
And love the high embowèd roof,
With antique pillars' massy proof,
And storied windows richly dight,
Casting a dim religious light.
There let the pealing organ blow,
To the full-voiced choir below,
In service high, and anthems clear,
As may with sweetness, through mine ear,
Dissolve me into ecstasies,
And bring all Heav'n before mine eyes.
And may at last my weary age
Find out the peaceful hermitage,
The hairy gown and mossy cell,
Where I may sit and rightly spell,
Of every star that heav'n doth show,
And every herb that sips the dew;
Till old experience do attain
To something like prophetic strain.
These pleasures Melancholy give,
And I with thee will choose to live.

Lines from An Epitaph on the Marchioness of Winchester

Written in the spring of 1631, following the death of the 23-year-old marchioness on 15 April, giving birth to a stillborn son. First published in the 1645 collection.

Gentle lady may thy grave
Peace and quiet ever have;
After this thy travail sore
Sweet rest seize thee evermore,
That to give the world increase,
Shortened hast thy own life's lease;
Here, besides the sorrowing
That thy noble house doth bring,
Here be tears of perfect moan
Wept for thee in Helicon,[1]
And some flowers, and some bays,
For thy hearse to strew the ways,
Sent thee from the banks of Came,[2]
Devoted to thy virtuous name;
Whilst thou bright saint high sitt'st in glory,
Next her much like to thee in story,
That fair Syrian shepherdess,[3]
Who after years of barrenness,
The highly favoured Joseph bore
To him that served for her before,
And at her next birth much like thee,
Through pangs fled to felicity,

1. Helicon is a mountain sacred to the Muses.
2. Came is the River Cam in Cambridge.
3. The Syrian shepherdess is Rachel, wife of Jacob and mother of Joseph and Benjamin, whose birth killed her.

Far within the bosom bright
Of blazing majesty and light;
There with thee, new-welcome saint,
Like fortunes may her soul acquaint,
With thee there clad in radiant sheen,
No marchioness, but now a queen.

The Professional Poet

Lines from A Masque Presented at Ludlow Castle (*always known as* Comus)

The masque was developed in England in the sixteenth century and became the standard form of Court entertainment in the seventeenth, in which courtiers of both sexes performed. They were often devised by distinguished poets and dramatists. Milton wrote his while living in Hammersmith in 1633 at the suggestion of his friend, the composer Henry Lawes, with whom he had already collaborated on a musical entertainment, *Arcades*, in honour of Alice, Dowager Countess of Derby. Milton invented his wicked magician, Comus, ingeniously making him the son of Bacchus and Circe. *Comus* was written for the Earl of Bridgewater, whose children were pupils of Lawes, and they were the first performers on 29 September 1634. The text was published anonymously in 1637.

> *Comus.* The star that bids the shepherd fold,
> Now the top of heav'n doth hold,
> And the gilded car of day,
> His glowing axle doth allay
> In the steep Atlantic stream,
> And the slope sun his upward beam
> Shoots against the dusky pole,
> Pacing toward the other goal
> Of his chamber in the east.
> Meanwhile welcome joy, and feast,
> Midnight shout, and revelry,
> Tipsy dance, and jollity.
> Braid your locks with rosy twine,
> Dropping odours, dropping wine.

Rigour now is gone to bed,
And Advice with scrupulous head,
Strict Age, and sour Severity
With their grave saws in slumber lie.
We that are of purer fire,
Imitate the starry choir,
Who in their nightly watchful spheres,
Lead in swift round the months and years.
The sounds, and seas with all their finny drove,
Now to the moon in wavering morris move,
And on the tawny sands and shelves,
Trip the pert fairies and the dapper elves;
By dimpled brook, and fountain brim,
The wood-nymphs decked with daisies trim,
Their merry wakes, and pastimes keep:
What hath night to do with sleep?
Night hath better sweets to prove,
Venus now wakes, and wakens Love.
Come let us our rites begin
'Tis only daylight that makes sin . . .

Comus, pretending to be a shepherd, offers to guide the
Lady, lost in the wood. Her brothers are seeking her, and
the elder insists that her virtue will protect her from any
harm.

Elder Brother. Virtue could see to do what virtue would
By her own radiant light, though sun and moon
Were in the flat sea sunk. And Wisdom's self
Oft seeks to sweet retired solitude,
Where with her best nurse Contemplation
She plumes her feathers, and lets grow her wings
That in the various bustle of resort

Were all to-ruffled, and sometimes impaired.
He that has light within his own clear breast
May sit i' the centre, and enjoy bright day . . .

The Lady, offered a feast by Comus, rejects it and gives
her reasons.

> *The Lady.* If every just man that now pines with want
> Had but a moderate and beseeming share
> Of that which lewdly-pampered Luxury
> Now heaps upon some few with vast excess,
> Nature's full blessings would be well-dispensed
> In unsuperfluous even proportion
> And she no whit encumbered with her store;
> And then the Giver would be better thanked,
> His praise due paid, for swinish gluttony
> Ne'er looks to Heav'n amidst his gorgeous feast,
> But with besotted base ingratitude
> Crams, and blasphemes his feeder. Shall I go on?
> Or have I said enough?

Sabrina, the virgin goddess of the River Severn, is asked
to help the Lady escape from Comus.

Song

Sabrina fair
  Listen where thou art sitting
Under the glassy, cool, translucent wave,
  In twisted braids of lilies knitting
The loose train of thy amber-dropping hair;
   Listen for dear honour's sake,
   Goddess of the silver lake,
    Listen and save.

On Time

This is Milton at his most baroque. The whole poem is in two sentences, a rolling litany of the failings of Time and the joys of Eternity, the poet's vision set out in passionate, exclamatory, extravagant and splendid verse. It was written in 1633 and first published in the 1645 collection.

Fly envious Time, till thou run out thy race,
Call on the lazy leaden-stepping hours,
Whose speed is but the heavy plummet's pace;
And glut thyself with what thy womb devours,
Which is no more than what is false and vain,
And merely mortal dross;
So little is our loss,
So little is thy gain.
For when as each thing bad thou hast entombed,
And last of all, thy greedy self consumed,
Then long eternity shall greet our bliss
With an individual kiss;
And joy shall overtake us as a flood,
When everything that is sincerely good
And perfectly divine,
With Truth, and Peace, and Love shall ever shine
About the súpreme throne
Of him, t' whose happy-making sight alone,
When once our Heav'nly-guided soul shall climb,
Then all this earthy grossness quit,
Attired with stars, we shall for ever sit,
    Triumphing over Death, and Chance, and thee O Time.

At a Solemn Music

Milton suggests that human singing allows us to imagine heavenly singing, the 'bright seraphim', 'angel trumpets' and 'harps of golden wires', and introduces the idea he took up again in *Paradise Lost*: that all creatures, angelic and human, made music together before the fall of man. This poem also was written in 1633 and first published in the 1645 collection.

> Blest pair of Sirens,[1] pledges of Heav'n's joy,
> Sphere-borne harmonious sisters, Voice, and Verse,
> Wed your divine sounds, and mixed power employ
> Dead things[2] with inbreathed sense able to pierce,
> And to our high-raised fantasy present,
> That undisturbèd song of pure concent,[3]
> Ay sung before the sapphire-coloured throne
> To him that sits thereon
> With saintly shout, and solemn jubilee,
> Where the bright Seraphim in burning row
> Their loud uplifted angel trumpets blow,
> And the Cherubic host in thousand choirs
> Touch their immortal harps of golden wires,
> With those just spirits that wear victorious palms,
> Hymns devout and holy psalms
> Singing everlastingly;
> That we on earth with undiscording voice
> May rightly answer that melodious noise;

1. The Sirens are an allusion to Plato's *Republic*, in which singing Sirens are imagined to be part of the structure of the universe.

2. By 'Dead things' he means inanimate objects, for example, rocks.

3. 'concent' means harmony.

As once we did, till disproportioned sin
Jarred against Nature's chime, and with harsh din
Broke the fair music that all creatures made
To their great Lord, whose love their motion swayed
In perfect diapason, whilst they stood
In first obedience, and their state of good.
O may we soon again renew that song,
And keep in tune with Heav'n, till God ere long
To his celestial consort us unite,
To live with him, and sing in endless morn of light.

Lines *from* Lycidas

An elegy for a Cambridge friend, Edward King, drowned
in the Irish Sea, this was written in 1637 and first printed
in a volume of memorial verses published in 1638.
Modelled on the classical pastoral elegy, it presents King
and Milton as shepherds.

Yet once more, O ye laurels, and once more
Ye myrtles brown, with ivy never sere,
I come to pluck your berries harsh and crude,
And with forced fingers rude,
Shatter your leaves before the mellowing year.
Bitter constraint, and sad occasion dear,
Compels me to disturb your season due:
For Lycidas is dead, dead ere his prime,
Young Lycidas, and hath not left his peer.
Who would not sing for Lycidas? he knew
Himself to sing, and build the lofty rhyme.
He must not float upon his wat'ry bier
Unwept, and welter to the parching wind,
Without the meed of some melodious tear.
 Begin then, Sisters of the sacred well,
That from beneath the seat of Jove[1] doth spring;
Begin, and somewhat loudly sweep the string.
Hence with denial vain, and coy excuse;
So may some gentle Muse
With lucky words favour my destined urn,
And as he passes, turn
And bid fair peace be to my sable shroud.

1. The seat of Jove is Mount   ('Sisters') danced and sang.
Helicon, where the Muses

For we were nursed upon the self-same hill,
Fed the same flock, by fountain, shade, and rill.

Together both, ere the high lawns appeared
Under the opening eye-lids of the morn,
We drove afield, and both together heard
What time the grey-fly winds her sultry horn,
Batt'ning our flocks with the fresh dews of night,
Oft till the star that rose, at evening, bright
Toward heav'n's descent had sloped his westering wheel.
Meanwhile the rural ditties were not mute,
Tempered to th' oaten flute,
Rough satyrs danced, and fauns with cloven heel
From the glad sound would not be absent long,
And old Damoetas[2] loved to hear our song.

But O the heavy change, now thou art gone,
Now thou art gone, and never must return!
Thee shepherd, thee the woods, and desert caves,
With wild thyme and the gadding vine o'ergrown,
And all their echoes mourn.
The willows, and the hazel copses green,
Shall now no more be seen,
Fanning their joyous leaves to thy soft lays.
As killing as the canker to the rose,
Or taint-worm to the weanling herds that graze,
Or frost to flowers, that their gay wardrobe wear,
When first the whitethorn blows;
Such, Lycidas, thy loss to shepherd's ear.

Where were ye nymphs when the remorseless deep
Closed o'er the head of your loved Lycidas?
For neither were ye playing on the steep,

2. Damoetas, a classical name, may   King's tutors.
be meant for one of Milton and

Where your old Bards, the famous Druids lie,
Nor on the shaggy top of Mona[3] high,
Nor yet where Deva spreads her wizard stream:
Ay me, I fondly dream!
Had ye been there – for what could that have done?
What could the Muse herself that Orpheus bore,
The Muse herself, for her enchanting son
Whom universal nature did lament,
When by the rout that made the hideous roar,
His gory visage down the stream was sent,
Down the swift Hebrus to the Lesbian shore.[4]

Alas! What boots it with uncessant care
To tend the homely slighted shepherd's trade,
And strictly meditate the thankless Muse?
Were it not better done as others use,
To sport with Amaryllis in the shade,
Or with the tangles of Neaera's hair?
Fame is the spur that the clear spirit doth raise
(That last infirmity of noble mind)
To scorn delights, and live laborious days;
But the fair guerdon when we hope to find,
And think to burst out into sudden blaze,
Comes the blind Fury with th' abhorrèd shears,
And slits the thin-spun life. But not the praise,
Phoebus replied, and touched my trembling ears;
Fame is no plant that grows on mortal soil,
Nor in the glistering foil
Set off to th' world, nor in broad rumour lies,
But lives and spreads aloft by those pure eyes
And perfect witness of all-judging Jove;

3. Mona is the mountain home of the Druids, Deva is the River Dee.

4. Orpheus was torn to bits by the Maenads.

As he pronounces lastly on each deed,
Of so much fame in Heav'n expect thy meed.

. . .

Return, Alpheus,[5] the dread voice is past,
That shrunk thy streams; return, Sicilian Muse,
And call the vales, and bid them hither cast
Their bells, and flow'rets of a thousand hues
Ye valleys low, where the mild whispers use
Of shades, and wanton winds, and gushing brooks,
On whose fresh lap the swart star sparely looks,
Throw hither all your quaint enamelled eyes,
That on the green turf suck the honied showers,
And purple all the ground with vernal flowers.
Bring the rathe primrose that forsaken dies,
The tufted crow-toe, and pale jessamine,
The white pink, and the pansy freaked with jet,
The growing violet,
The musk-rose, and the well-attired woodbine,
With cowslips wan that hang the pensive head,
And every flower that sad embroidery wears:
Bid amaranthus all his beauty shed,
And daffadillies fill their cups with tears,
To strew the laureate hearse where Lycid lies
For so to interpose a little ease,
Let our frail thoughts daily with false surmise,
Ay me! whilst thee the shores, and sounding seas
Wash far away, where'er thy bones are hurled,

5. Alpheus is a river associated with pastoral poetry.

Whether beyond the stormy Hebrides,
Where thou perhaps under the whelming tide
Visit'st the bottom of the monstrous world;
Or whether thou to our moist vows denied,
Sleep'st by the fable of Bellerus[6] old,
Where the great vision of the guarded mount
Looks toward Namancos and Bayona's hold;[7]
Look homeward angel now, and melt with ruth.
And, O ye dolphins, waft the hapless youth.

    Weep no more, woeful shepherds, weep no more,
For Lycidas your sorrow is not dead,
Sunk though he be beneath the wat'ry floor,
So sinks the day-star in the ocean bed,
And yet anon repairs his drooping head,
And tricks his beams, and with new-spangled ore,
Flames in the forehead of the morning sky:
So Lycidas sunk low, but mounted high,
Through the dear might of him that walked the waves,
Where other groves, and other streams along,
With nectar pure his oozy locks he laves,
And hears the unexpressive nuptial song,
In the blest kingdoms meek of joy and love.
There entertain him all the saints above,
In solemn troops, and sweet societies
That sing, and singing in their glory move,
And wipe the tears for ever from his eyes.

6. Bellerus is an invention of Milton, representing Land's End.
7. Namancos and Bayona are Spanish places representing the threat of Roman Catholicism.

Now, Lycidas, the shepherds weep no more;
Henceforth thou art the Genius of the shore
In thy large recompense, and shalt be good
To all that wander in that perilous flood.
    Thus sang the uncouth swain to th' oaks and rills,
While the still Morn went out with sandals grey;
He touched the tender stops of various quills,
With eager thought warbling his Doric lay;[8]
And now the sun had stretched out all the hills,
And now was dropped into the western bay;
At last he rose, and twitched his mantle blue:
Tomorrow to fresh woods and pastures new.

8. Doric was the language of the Greek pastoral poets.

The Sonnets

The sonnets make up a special group among Milton's poems. They are some of his most private and also his most public utterances, and they were written very occasionally over a period of nearly thirty years. There are twenty-four in all, of which I have selected twelve, half of them purely personal, two humorous, three eulogies of great contemporaries incorporating political and religious messages, and one thunderous outcry against a religiously inspired massacre.

'O nightingale, that on yon bloomy spray'

His earliest sonnet in English, and the most conventional, written about 1629 when he was at Cambridge and producing Italian sonnets describing his experience of falling in love. It is a delicious young man's declaration, and he liked it enough to print it in his first collection in 1645.

O nightingale, that on yon bloomy spray
   Warblest at eve, when all the woods are still,
   Thou with fresh hope the lover's heart dost fill,
   While the jolly Hours lead on propitious May;
Thy liquid notes that close the eye of day,
   First heard before the shallow cuckoo's bill[1]
   Portend success in love; O if Jove's will
   Have linked that amorous power to thy soft lay,
Now timely sing, ere the rude bird of hate
   Foretell my hopeless doom in some grove nigh:
   As thou from year to year hast sung too late
For my relief, yet hadst no reason why:
   Whether the Muse, or Love call thee his mate,
   Both them I serve, and of their train am I.

1. The cuckoo is the 'bird of hate'. It was believed that hearing the cuckoo before the nightingale brought bad luck to a lover.

'How soon hath Time the subtle thief of youth'

This carefully thought-out sonnet, also written when Milton was in residence at Cambridge, and before he had published anything, was sent in a letter to a friend. He writes of his failure to achieve anything, jokes about his youthful appearance and calmly asserts his confidence in his future under the eye of God. It was first published in his 1645 collection.

How soon hath Time the subtle thief of youth,
    Stol'n on his wing my three and twentieth year!
    My hasting days fly on with full career,
    But my late spring no bud or blossom shew'th.
Perhaps my semblance might deceive the truth,
    That I to manhood am arrived so near,
    And inward ripeness doth much less appear,
    That some more timely-happy spirits endu'th.
Yet be it less or more, or soon or slow,
    It shall be still in strictest measure even,
    To that same lot, however mean, or high,
Toward which Time leads me, and the will of Heaven;
    All is, if I have grace to use it so,
    As ever in my great task-master's eye.

When the Assault was Intended to the City

Early in the Civil War, in November 1642, the royalist army reached Brentford on the outskirts of London, sacked it, and threatened the metropolis itself, which was solidly for Parliament. Milton, a staunch Parliamentarian, was living in Aldersgate with his two nephews and pupils, and this partly comical sonnet may have been written to amuse and instruct the boys with tales from Plutarch. It is ostensibly addressed to the King's officers, reminding them that it is wiser not to attack the house of a poet. Plutarch wrote of the Emathian conqueror, Alexander, who chose to spare the house of the poet Pindar when he took Thebes. Euripides is 'sad Electra's poet': a song from his play softened the hearts of the Spartans and Thebans when they defeated Athens in 404 BC, and they decided not to destroy the city of so great a poet. In fact a defending army of the London trained bands, led by the Earl of Essex, faced the royalists at Turnham Green, and they withdrew. The sonnet was published in the 1645 collection.

Captain or colonel, or knight in arms,
    Whose chance on these defenceless doors may seize,
    If deed of honour did thee ever please,
    Guard them, and him within protect from harms;
He can requite thee, for he knows the charms
    That call fame on such gentle acts as these,
    And he can spread thy name o'er lands and seas,
    Whatever clime the sun's bright circle warms.

Lift not thy spear against the Muses' bower:
    The great Emathian conqueror bid spare
    The house of Pindarus, when temple and tower
Went to the ground; and the repeated air
    Of sad Electra's poet had the power
    To save th' Athenian walls from ruin bare.

'A book was writ of late called *Tetrachordon*'

This is another joking sonnet, in which he shows off his learning and verbal dexterity. He had written several pamphlets on the subject of divorce, and in 1645 one called *Tetrachordon* appeared. The word means 'four-stringed' in Greek, and alludes to four passages in the Bible invoked by Milton. The sonnet, written in 1647, pictures readers browsing at a book stall, unable to deal with the difficult title and struggling with it for hours – for the time it would take to walk as far as Mile-End Green, i.e., right out of town. The Scottish names are there to raise a laugh. Quintilian, a Roman critic of the first century AD, was much cited by Renaissance scholars such as Sir John Cheke, the first Regius Professor of Greek at Cambridge, who tutored the young Edward VI, and these three renowned figures bring the sonnet to its striking close. It was not published until 1673.

A book was writ of late called *Tetrachordon*;
    And woven close, both matter, form and style;
    The subject new: it walked the town a while,
    Numb'ring good intellects; now seldom pored on.
Cries the stall-reader, Bless us! what a word on
    A title page is this! and some in file
    Stand spelling false, while one might walk to Mile-
    End Green. Why is it harder sirs than Gordon,
Colkitto, or Macdonnel, or Galasp?
    Those rugged names to our like mouths grow sleek
    That would have made Quintilian stare and gasp.

Thy age, like ours, O soul of Sir John Cheke,
   Hated not learning worse than toad or asp,
   When thou taught'st Cambridge and King Edward
                                 Greek.

On the Lord General Fairfax at the Siege of Colchester

The siege of Colchester lasted for two and a half months in the summer of 1648, when this sonnet was written. It was a brutal business: the town was starved into surrender, and two royalist leaders were shot on Sir Thomas Fairfax's orders. He had been known for his personal heroism, pre-eminent among Cromwell's generals, and no doubt the royalist risings in Kent, Wales and Scotland in 1648 led to his cruel action. The following year, after the execution of the King, of which he disapproved, he retired into private life. His daughter was tutored by Milton's friend and fellow poet Andrew Marvell. The sonnet, unpublished in Milton's lifetime, was first printed in *Letters of State* – an edition of his writings and a short biography by his nephew Edward Phillips – in 1694.

Fairfax, whose name in arms through Europe rings
   Filling each mouth with envy, or with praise,
   And all her jealous monarchs with amaze,
   And rumours loud, that daunt remotest kings,
Thy firm unshaken virtue ever brings
   Victory home, though new rebellions raise
   Their Hydra heads, and the false North[1] displays
   Her broken league, to imp their serpent wings,
O yet a nobler task awaits thy hand;
   For what can war, but endless war still breed,
   Till truth, and right from violence be freed,

---

1. 'false North', i.e., the Scots.

And public faith cleared from the shameful brand
  Of public fraud.[2] In vain doth valour bleed
While avarice, and rapine share the land.

To the Lord General Cromwell,
May 1652
On the Proposals of Certain Ministers of the Committee for Propagation of the Gospel

Milton alludes to three of Cromwell's victories against the Scots (Preston, Dunbar and Worcester) before urging him to withstand Parliament, which had resolved to keep some form of the Established Church. Cromwell himself favoured a disestablished Church, and Milton is voicing his support. Like the Fairfax sonnet, it was first published in 1694 by Milton's nephew.

> Cromwell, our chief of men, who through a cloud
>   Not of war only, but detractions rude,
>   Guided by faith and matchless fortitude
>   To peace and truth thy glorious way hast ploughed,
> And on the neck of crownèd Fortune proud
>   Hast reared God's trophies and his work pursued,
>   While Darwen stream with blood of Scots imbrued,
>   And Dunbar field resounds thy praises loud,
> And Worcester's laureate wreath; yet much remains
>   To conquer still; peace hath her victories
>   No less renowned than war, new foes arise
> Threat'ning to bind our souls with secular chains:
>   Help us to save free conscience from the paw
>   Of hireling wolves whose Gospel is their maw.

To Sir Henry Vane the Younger

'Vane, young in years' was thirty-nine when the sonnet was written. He was a remarkable figure, a gifted administrator who served as Governor of Massachusetts in 1635 and in England during the interregnum on the Navy Board and the Council of State. He was a close friend of Cromwell, and an advocate of complete religious toleration. He was also an idealist who fell out with people. Although he did not approve the execution of the King, Charles II considered him a dangerous man, and in 1662 he was executed on a trumped-up charge. He spoke bravely on the scaffold. This sonnet first appeared in the year of his death, in a memoir, with a note saying Milton had sent it to Vane in July 1652.

> Vane, young in years, but in sage counsel old,
>   Than whom a better senator ne'er held
>   The helm of Rome, when gowns not arms repelled
>   The fierce Epirot[1] and the African bold:
> Whether to settle peace or to unfold
>   The drift of hollow states, hard to be spelled,
>   Then to advise how war may best, upheld,
>   Move by her two main nerves, iron and gold,
> In all her equipage; besides to know
>   Both spiritual power and civil, what each means,
>   What severs each, thou hast learnt, which few have
>   done.

1. 'The fierce Epirot' is King Pyrrhus of Epirus and 'the African' is Hannibal, both of whom were effectively dealt with by the civilian Roman Senators – i.e., gowned, not armed – who refused to ransom Hannibal's Roman prisoners.

The bounds of either sword[2] to thee we owe;
Therefore on thy firm hand religion leans
In peace, and reckons thee her eldest son.

2. 'either sword': meaning the two powers of state and Church.

'When I consider how my light is spent'

Written in 1652, the year in which Milton became blind, this sonnet is an admonishment to himself to bear God's 'light yoke' patiently. The thousands who speed at God's bidding are the angels and archangels who will make their appearance in *Paradise Lost*. First published in 1673.

When I consider how my light is spent,
    Ere half my days, in this dark world and wide,
    And that one talent which is death to hide,
    Lodged with me useless, though my soul more bent
To serve therewith my Maker, and present
    My true account, lest he returning chide,
    Doth God exact day labour, light denied,
    I fondly ask; but patience to prevent
That murmur, soon replies, God doth not need
    Either man's work or his own gifts; who best
    Bear his mild yoke, they serve him best; his state
Is kingly. Thousands at his bidding speed
    And post o'er land and ocean without rest:
    They also serve who only stand and wait.

On the Late Massacre in Piedmont

The Vaudois were a Protestant sect founded in the twelfth century, simple people living remotely and peacefully in the Alps on the borders of France and Italy. In 1655 they were attacked under the orders of the Catholic Duke of Savoy and expelled from their villages, with nearly 2,000 of them butchered. Cromwell took up their cause, complained to the Catholic rulers, and sent money and a special envoy; and Milton was inspired to this glorious protest. First published in 1673.

Avenge O Lord thy slaughtered saints, whose bones
    Lie scattered on the Alpine mountains cold;
    Ev'n them who kept thy truth so pure of old
    When all our fathers worshipped stocks and stones,
Forget not: in thy book record their groans
    Who were thy sheep and in their ancient fold
    Slain by the bloody Piedmontese that rolled
    Mother with infant down the rocks. Their moans
The vales redoubled to the hills, and they
    To Heav'n. Their martyred blood and ashes sow
    O'er all th' Italian fields where still doth sway
The triple Tyrant:[1] that from these may grow
A hundredfold, who having learnt thy way
Early may fly the Babylonian woe.[2]

1. The 'triple Tyrant' is the Pope, whose crown has three tiers.
2. Protestants identified the Babylon of the Book of Revelation with Roman Catholicism.

'Lawrence of virtuous father virtuous son'

The sonnet was written in the 1650s, addressed to a young friend, Edward Lawrence, who became an MP at the age of twenty-three in 1656 and died the following year. He was the son of Henry Lawrence, President of Cromwell's Council of State and a frequent visitor to the house into which Milton moved with his family in 1651, when he was appointed Latin Secretary to the Council. In this year Milton's wife was pregnant and caring for their baby son and two daughters, and she and the baby boy both died the next summer of 1652, so it is unlikely the poem was written until later. His description of the pleasures to be had in dining with a congenial friend and enjoying wine and music together clearly looks back to Horace's treatment of the same theme. First published in 1673.

Lawrence of virtuous father virtuous son,
    Now that the fields are dank, and ways are mire,
    Where shall we sometimes meet, and by the fire
    Help waste a sullen day, what may be won
From the hard season gaining? Time will run
    On smoother, till Favonius[1] re-inspire
    The frozen earth; and clothe in fresh attire
    The lily and rose, that neither sowed nor spun.
What neat repast shall feast us, light and choice,

---

1. Favonius is the Latin name for the west wind.

Of Attic[2] taste, with wine, whence we may rise
  To hear the lute well touched, or artful voice
Warble immortal notes and Tuscan air?
  He who of those delights can judge, and spare
To interpose them oft, is not unwise.

2. Attic means, literally, Athenian, and suggests
refinement, moderation and good taste.

To Mr Cyriack Skinner upon his Blindness

Cyriack Skinner (1627–1700) was a pupil of Milton in the 1640s, becoming a close friend and later a supporter through difficult times. He was a grandson of Edward Coke, Chief Justice under James I, who fought the King and the Church to preserve the independence of the judicial system, and he is believed to be the author of the anonymous biography of Milton in the Bodleian. This sonnet was written about 1655 and first published in *Letters of State* in 1694.

Cyriack, this three years' day these eyes, though clear
    To outward view, of blemish or of spot,
    Bereft of light their seeing have forgot,
    Nor to their idle orbs doth sight appear
Of sun or moon or star throughout the year,
    Or man or woman. Yet I argue not
    Against Heaven's hand or will, nor bate a jot
    Of heart or hope; but still bear up and steer
Right onward. What supports me doth thou ask?
    The conscience, friend, to have lost them overplied
    In liberty's defence, my noble task,
Of which all Europe talks from side to side.
    This thought might lead me through the world's vain
                              masque
    Content though blind, had I no better guide.

'Methought I saw my late espousèd saint'

This last and most beautiful of Milton's sonnets speaks of his second wife, Katherine, who died after giving birth to her first child, and was probably written in 1658. There are several versions of the Greek myth of Alcestis, who offered her own life to save that of her husband, King Admetus, and in one she descended to the underworld and was then brought back by Hercules, 'Jove's great son'. First published in 1673.

Methought I saw my late espousèd saint
    Brought to me like Alcestis from the grave,
    Whom Jove's great son to her glad husband gave,
    Rescued from death by force though pale and faint.
Mine as whom washed from spot of child-bed taint
    Purification in the old Law[1] did save,
    And such, as yet once more I trust to have
    Full sight of her in Heaven without restraint,
Came vested all in white, pure as her mind:
    Her face was veiled, yet to my fancied sight,
    Love, sweetness, goodness, in her person shined
So clear, as in no face with more delight.
    But O as to embrace me she inclined,
    I waked, she fled, and day brought back my night.

1. Refers to Leviticus, in which a woman who has given birth to a son is deemed unclean for forty days; if she gives birth to a daughter, she is unclean for eighty days.

The Last Years

Lines from Paradise Lost

Blank verse had been used in English before, first by the Earl of Surrey in his translation of part of the *Aeneid* in 1540, and then by the Elizabethan and Jacobean playwrights, and supremely by Shakespeare. Milton wrote a short introduction to the second edition of his poem in which he characterized the form as 'English heroic verse without rhyme, as that of Homer in Greek, and of Virgil in Latin; rhyme being no necessary adjunct or true ornament of poem or good verse, in longer works especially, but the invention of barbarous age, to set off wretched matter and lame metre'. He ended by claiming that he was setting an example and recovering an ancient liberty by giving up 'the troublesome and modern bondage of rhyming'.

His epic tells the story of the creation, of the first man and woman, Adam and Eve, and their expulsion from the Garden of Eden. A dramatic villain-hero, Satan, is given to soliloquizing, as in a Jacobean tragedy. Satan is the angel who rebels against God's authority and is driven out of Heaven with his supporters. He avenges himself by corrupting man.

Paradise Lost was a long-planned project, originally intended as a dramatic tragedy. Milton reached the decision to make it an epic poem by 1658, when he probably began to have it written down. He composed in his head during the night and in the morning dictated as many as forty lines from memory to whoever was available to take them down, discarding and correcting later. His nephew Edward Phillips, who was one of his assistants, described this process and said the whole poem was written between 1658 and 1663. It was first published in ten books, redrafted by Milton himself in twelve for the second edition.

At three points in the narrative Milton speaks of himself and the circumstances of his composition. They come in Book III, lines 40–55, where he hails God not only as the creator of light but as light itself, and mourns his own blindness:

>   ... Thus with the year
> Seasons return, but not to me returns
> Day, or the sweet approach of ev'n or morn,
> Or sight of vernal bloom, or summer's rose,
> Or flocks, or herds, or human face divine;
> But cloud instead, and ever-during dark
> Surrounds me, from the cheerful ways of men
> Cut off, and for the Book of Knowledge fair
> Presented with a universal blank
> Of Nature's works to me expunged and razed,
> And wisdom at one entrance quite shut out.
> So much the rather thou celestial Light
> Shine inward, and the mind through all her powers
> Irradiate, there plant eyes, all mist from thence
> Purge and disperse, that I may see and tell
> Of things invisible to mortal sight.

At the start of Book VII, line 25, he writes of being visited by Urania, whom he describes as a Christian Muse, inspiring him and carrying him up to Heaven and back to Earth, even though he has 'fallen on evil days' and 'evil tongues':

In darkness, and with dangers compassed round,
And solitude; yet not alone, while thou
Visit'st my slumbers nightly, or when Morn
Purples the east: still govern thou my song,
Urania, and fit audience find, though few.

Again, in Book IX, lines 21–6, he invokes Urania, his
'celestial patroness':

                              . . . who deigns
Her nightly visitation unimplored,
And dictates to me slumb'ring, or inspires
Easy my unpremeditated verse:
Since first this subject for heroic song
Pleased me long choosing, and beginning late . . .

In Book I he establishes the character of Satan. In lines
254–64 Satan is speaking from the floor of Hell, address-
ing his fellow rebel angels and weighing up his and their
position since they have been expelled from Heaven and
forced to settle in Hell.

The mind is its own place, and in itself
Can make a Heav'n of Hell, a Hell of Heav'n.
What matter where, if I be still the same,
And what I should be, all but less than he
Whom thunder hath made greater? Here at least
We shall be free; th' Almighty hath not built
Here for his envy, will not drive us hence:
Here we may reign secure, and in my choice
To reign is worth ambition though in Hell:
Better to reign in Hell, than serve in Heav'n.

The rebel angels are shown building their 'high capital',
or palace of Pandaemonium.

   There stood a hill not far whose grisly top
Belched fire and rolling smoke; the rest entire
Shone with a glossy scurf, undoubted sign
That in his womb was hid metallic ore,
The work of sulphur. Thither winged with speed
A numerous brígade hastened. As when bands
Of pioneers with spade and pickaxe armed
Forerun the royal camp, to trench a field
Or cast a rampart. Mammon led them on,
Mammon, the least erected Spirit that fell
From Heav'n, for ev'n in Heav'n his looks and thoughts
Were always downward bent, admiring more
The riches of Heav'n's pavement, trodden gold,
Than aught divine or holy else enjoyed
In vision beatific: by him first
Men also, and by his suggestion taught,
Ransacked the centre, and with impious hands
Rifled the bowels of their mother Earth
For treasures better hid. Soon had his crew
Opened into the hill a spacious wound
And digged out ribs of gold. Let none admire
That riches grow in Hell; that soil may best
Deserve the precious bane. And here let those
Who boast in mortal things, and wond'ring tell
Of Babel, and the works of Memphian[1] kings,
Learn how their greatest monuments of fame,

1. Memphis was the old name for
Cairo (Alcairo), Memphians are
Egyptians, and their works the
Pyramids.

And strength and art are easily outdone
By Spirits reprobate, and in an hour
What in an age they with incessant toil
And hands innumerable scarce perform.
Nigh on the plain in many cells prepared,
That underneath had veins of liquid fire
Sluiced from the lake, a second multitude
With wondrous art founded the massy ore,
Severing each kind, and scummed the bullion dross:
A third as soon had formed within the ground
A various mould, and from the boiling cells
By strange conveyance filled each hollow nook,
As in an organ from one blast of wind
To many a row of pipes the sound-board breathes.
Anon out of the earth a fabric huge
Rose like an exhalation, with the sound
Of dulcet symphonies and voices sweet,
Built like a temple, where pilasters round
Were set, and Doric pillars overlaid
With golden architrave; nor did there want
Cornice or frieze with bossy sculptures grav'n;
The roof was fretted gold. Not Babylon,[2]
Nor great Alcairo such magnificence
Equalled in all their glories, to enshrine
Belus or Serapis their gods, or seat
Their kings, when Egypt with Assyria strove
In wealth and luxury. Th' ascending pile
Stood fixed her stately heighth, and straight the doors
Op'ning their brazen folds discover wide
Within, her ample spaces, o'er the smooth
And level pavement: from the archèd roof
Pendent by subtle magic many a row

2. Babylon and Alcairo were great heathen cities.

Of starry lamps and blazing cressets fed
With naphtha and asphaltus yielded light
As from a sky. The hasty multitude
Admiring entered, and the work some praise
And some the architect: his hand was known
In Heav'n by many a towered structure high,
Where sceptred angels held their residence,
And sat as princes, whom the súpreme King
Exalted to such power, and gave to rule,
Each in his hierarchy, the orders bright.
Nor was his name unheard or unadored
In ancient Greece; and in Ausonian land[3]
Men called him Mulciber;[4] and how he fell
From Heav'n, they fabled, thrown by angry Jove
Sheer o'er the crystal battlements: from morn
To noon he fell, from noon to dewy eve,
A summer's day: and with the setting sun
Dropped from the zenith like a falling star,
On Lemnos th' Aégean isle: thus they relate,
Erring; for he with this rebellious rout
Fell long before; nor aught availed him now
To have built in Heav'n high tow'rs; nor did he 'scape
By all his engines, but was headlong sent
With his industrious crew to build in Hell.

3. The Ausonian land was the
Greek name for Italy.
4. Mulciber is another name for
Hephaistos (Greek name) or Vulcan

(Latin name), who, according to
some legends, built the palaces of
the gods before being thrown out
of Heaven.

Early in Book IV, Milton gives Satan a long soliloquy in which he meditates on his position, exiled from Heaven, and is forced to acknowledge that there is no possibility of returning to God's favour.

O had his powerful destiny ordained
Me some inferior angel, I had stood
Then happy, no unbounded hope had raised
Ambition. Yet why not? Some other Power
As great might have aspired, and me though mean
Drawn to his part; but other Powers as great
Fell not, but stand unshaken, from within
Or from without, to all temptations armed.
Hadst thou the same free will and power to stand?
Thou hadst: whom hast thou then or what to accuse,
But Heav'n's free lore dealt equally to all?
Be then his love accursed, since love or hate,
To me alike, it deals eternal woe.
Nay cursed be thou; since against his thy will
Chose freely what it now so justly rues.
Me miserable! Which way shall I fly
Infinite wrath, and infinite despair?
Which way I fly is Hell; myself am Hell;
And in the lowest deep a lower deep
Still threat'ning to devour me opens wide,
To which the Hell I suffer seems a Heav'n.

. . .

So farewell hope, and with hope farewell fear,
Farewell remorse: all good to me is lost;
Evil be thou my good; by thee at least
Divided empire with Heav'n's King I hold
By thee, and more than half perhaps will reign;
As man ere long, and this new world shall know.

Book IV, lines 288–365

Satan sees for the first time the Garden of Eden and
Adam and Eve among the other creatures.

Two of far nobler shape erect and tall,
Godlike erect, with native honour clad
In naked majesty seemed lords of all,
And worthy seemed, for in their looks divine
The image of their glorious Maker shone,
Truth, wisdom, sanctitude severe and pure,
Severe, but in true filial freedom placed;
Whence true authority in men; though both
Not equal, as their sex not equal seemed;
For contemplation he and valour formed,
For softness she and sweet attractive grace,
He for God only, she for God in him:
His fair large front and eye sublime declared
Absolute rule; and hyacinthine locks
Round from his parted forelock manly hung
Clust'ring, but not beneath his shoulders broad:
She as a veil down to the slender waist
Her unadornèd golden tresses wore
Dishevelled, but in wanton ringlets waved
As the vine curls her tendrils, which implied
Subjection, but required with gentle sway,

And by her yielded, by him best received,
Yielded with coy submission, modest pride,
And sweet reluctant amorous delay.
Nor those mysterious parts were then concealed;
Then was not guilty shame, dishonest shame
Of nature's works, honour dishonourable,
Sin-bred, how have ye troubled all mankind
With shows instead, mere shows of seeming pure,
And banished from man's life his happiest life,
Simplicity and spotless innocence.
So passed they naked on, nor shunned the sight
Of God or angel, for they thought no ill:
So hand in hand they passed, the loveliest pair
That ever since in love's embraces met,
Adam the goodliest man of men since born
His sons, the fairest of her daughters Eve.
Under a tuft of shade that on a green
Stood whispering soft, by a fresh fountain side
They sat them down, and after no more toil
Of their sweet gard'ning labour than sufficed
To recommend cool Zephyr, and made ease
More easy, wholesome thirst and appetite
More grateful, to their supper fruits they fell,
Nectarine fruits which the compliant boughs
Yielded them, sidelong as they sat recline
On the soft downy bank damasked with flow'rs:
The savoury pulp they chew, and in the rind
Still as they thirsted scoop the brimming stream;
Nor gentle purpose, nor endearing smiles
Wanted, nor youthful dalliance as beseems
Fair couple, linked in happy nuptial league,
Alone as they. About them frisking played
All beasts of th' earth, since wild, and of all chase
In wood or wilderness, forest or den;

Sporting the lion ramped, and in his paw
Dandled the kid; bears, tigers, ounces, pards
Gambolled before them, th' unwieldy elephant
To make them mirth used all his might, and wreathed
His lithe proboscis; close the serpent sly
Insinuating, wove with Gordian twine[1]
His braided train, and of his fatal guile
Gave proof unheeded; others on the grass
Couched, and now filled with pasture gazing sat,
Or bedward ruminating: for the sun
Declined was hasting now with prone career
To th' Ocean Isles,[2] and in th' ascending Scale
Of Heav'n the stars that usher evening rose:
When Satan still in gaze, as first he stood,
Scarce thus at length failed speech recovered sad.

O Hell! What do mine eyes with grief behold,
Into our room of bliss thus high advanced
Creatures of other mould, earth-born perhaps,
Not Spirits, yet to Heav'nly Spirits bright
Little inferior; whom my thoughts pursue
With wonder, and could love, so lively shines
In them divine resemblance, and such grace
The hand that formed them on their shape hath poured.
A gentle pair, ye little think how nigh
Your change approaches, when all these delights
Will vanish and deliver ye to woe . . .

1. The Gordian knot was cut by   2. The Ocean Isles are the Azores.
Alexander's sword.

Eve recalls her awakening to life and speaks to Adam, unaware of Satan watching and listening jealously.

That day I oft remember, when from sleep
I first awaked, and found myself reposed
Under a shade of flow'rs, much wond'ring where
And what I was, whence thither brought, and how.
Not distant far from thence a murmuring sound
Of waters issued from a cave and spread
Into a liquid plain, then stood unmoved
Pure as th' expanse of heav'n; I thither went
With unexperienced thought, and laid me down
On the green bank, to look into the clear
Smooth lake, that to me seemed another sky.
As I bent down to look, just opposite,
A shape within the wat'ry gleam appeared
Bending to look on me: I started back,
It started back, but pleased I soon returned,
Pleased it returned as soon with answering looks
Of sympathy and love; there I had fixed
Mine eyes till now, and pined with vain desire,
Had not a voice thus warned me, What thou seest,
What there thou seest fair creature is thyself,
With thee it came and goes: but follow me,
And I will bring thee where no shadow stays
Thy coming, and thy soft embraces, he
Whose image thou art, him thou shall enjoy
Inseparably thïne, to him shalt bear
Multitudes like thyself, and thence be called
Mother of human race: what could I do,
But follow straight, invisibly thus led?

Till I espied thee, fair indeed and tall,
Under a platan, yet methought less fair,
Less winning soft, less amiably mild,
Than that smooth wat'ry image; back I turned,
Thou following cried'st aloud, Return, fair Eve;
Whom fli'st thou? Whom thou fli'st, of him thou art,
His flesh, his bone; to give thee being I lent
Out of my side to thee, nearest my heart
Substantial life, to have thee by my side
Henceforth an individual solace dear;
Part of my soul I seek thee, and thee claim
My other half: with that thy gentle hand
Seized mine, I yielded, and from that time see
How beauty is excelled by manly grace
And wisdom, which alone is truly fair.

So spake our general mother, and with eyes
Of conjugal attraction unreproved,
And meek surrender, half embracing leaned
On our first father; half her swelling breast
Naked met his under the flowing gold
Of her loose tresses hid: he in delight
Both of her beauty and submissive charms
Smiled with superior love, as Jupiter
On Juno smiles, when he impregns the clouds
That shed May flowers; and pressed her matron lip
With kisses pure: aside the Devil turned
For envy, yet with jealous leer malign
Eyed them askance, and to himself thus plained.

Sight hateful, sight tormenting! Thus these two
Imparadised in one another's arms
The happier Eden, shall enjoy their fill
Of bliss on bliss, while I to Hell am thrust,

Where neither joy nor love, but fierce desire,
Among our other torments not the least,
Still unfulfilled with pain of longing pines . . .

Book IV, lines 598–609

Evening in Paradise.

Now came still ev'ning on, and twilight grey
Had in her sober livery all things clad;
Silence accompanied, for beast and bird,
They to their grassy couch, these to their nests
Were slunk, all but the wakeful nightingale;
She all night long her amorous descant sung;
Silence was pleased: now glowed the firmament
With living sapphires: Hesperus that led
The starry host, rode brightest, till the moon
Rising in clouded majesty, at length
Apparent queen unveiled her peerless light,
And o'er the dark her silver mantle threw.

Book IV, lines 678–88

Adam answers Eve's question as to why the moon and
stars shine at night while they are sleeping.

Millions of spiritual creatures walk the earth
Unseen, both when we wake, and when we sleep:
All these with ceaseless praise his works behold
Both day and night: how often from the steep

Of echoing hill or thicket have we heard
Celestial voices to the midnight air,
Sole, or responsive each to other's note
Singing their great Creator: oft in bands
While they keep watch, or nightly rounding walk
With Heav'nly touch of instrumental sounds
In full harmonic number joined, their songs
Divide the night, and lift our thoughts to Heaven.

Book IV, *lines 977–90*

The archangel Gabriel and the angels Ithuriel and
Zephon find Satan near Eve, threaten him and provoke
a fierce response and a virtuoso passage from Milton,
bringing together classical goddess and English plough-
man, the mountains of Tenerife and Atlas, and Satan
self-inflated like an angry toad.

While thus he spake, th' angelic squadron bright
Turned fiery red, sharp'ning in moonèd horns
Their phalanx, and began to hem him round
With ported spears, as thick as when a field
Of Ceres ripe for harvest waving bends
Her bearded grove of ears, which way the wind
Sways them; the careful ploughman doubting stands
Lest on the threshing floor his hopeful sheaves
Prove chaff. On th' other side Satan alarmed
Collecting all his might dilated stood,
Like Tenerife or Atlas unremoved:
His stature reached the sky, and on his crest
Sat horror plumed; nor wanted in his grasp
What seemed both spear and shield . . .

The archangel Raphael, sent by God to talk with Adam
and Eve, flies to the Garden of Eden. He warns them of
the danger they are in and reminds them to be obedient
to God's command. Adam and Eve prepare their first
dinner party for their guest.

At once on th' eastern cliff of Paradise
He lights, and to his proper shape returns
A Seraph winged; six wings he wore, to shade
His lineaments divine; the pair that clad
Each shoulder broad, came mantling o'er his breast
With regal ornament; the middle pair
Girt like a starry zone his waist, and round
Skirted his loins and thighs with downy gold
And colours dipped in Heav'n; the third his feet
Shadowed from either heel with feathered mail
Sky-tinctured grain. Like Maia's son[1] he stood,
And shook his plumes, that Heav'nly fragrance filled
The circuit wide. Straight knew him all the bands
Of angels under watch; and to his state,
And to his message high in honour rise;
For on some message high they guessed him bound.
Their glittering tents he passed, and now is come
Into the blissful field, through groves of myrrh,
And flow'ring odours, cassia, nard, and balm;
A wilderness of sweets; for Nature here
Wantoned as in her prime, and played at will
Her virgin fancies, pouring forth more sweet,
Wild above rule or art; enormous bliss.

---

1. Maia's son is Mercury, or Hermes.

Him through the spicy forest onward come
Adam discerned, as in the door he sat
Of his cool bow'r, while now the mounted sun
Shot down direct his fervid rays to warm
Earth's inmost womb, more warmth than Adam needs:
And Eve within, due at her hour prepared
For dinner savoury fruits, of taste to please
True appetite, and not disrelish thirst
Of nectarous draughts between, from milky stream,
Berry or grape: to whom thus Adam called.

    Haste hither Eve, and worth thy sight behold
Eastward among those trees, what glorious shape
Comes this way moving; seems another morn
Ris'n on mid-noon; some great behest from Heav'n
To us perhaps he brings, and will vouchsafe
This day to be our guest. But go with speed,
And what thy stores contain, bring forth and pour
Abundance, fit to honour and receive
Our Heav'nly stranger; well we may afford
Our givers their own gifts, and large bestow
From large bestowed, where Nature multiplies
Her fertile growth, and by disburd'ning grows
More fruitful, which instructs us not to spare.

    To whom thus Eve, Adam, earth's hallowed mould,
Of God inspired, small store will serve, where store,
All seasons, ripe for use hangs on the stalk;
Save what by frugal storing firmness gains
To nourish, and superfluous moist consumes:
But I will haste and from each bough and brake,
Each plant and juiciest gourd will pluck such choice
To entertain our angel guest, as he
Beholding shall confess that here on earth
God hath dispensed his bounties as in Heav'n.

    So saying, with dispatchful looks in haste

She turns, on hospitable thoughts intent
What choice to choose for delicacy best,
What order, so contrived as not to mix
Tastes, not well joined, inelegant, but bring
Taste after taste upheld with kindliest change;
Bestirs her then, and from each tender stalk
Whatever Earth all-bearing Mother yields
In India east or west, or middle shore
In Pontus or the Punic coast, or where
Alcinous reigned, fruit of all kinds, in coat,
Rough, or smooth rined, or bearded husk, or shell
She gathers, tribute large, and on the board
Heaps with unsparing hand; for drink the grape
She crushes, inoffensive must, and meaths
From many a berry, and from sweet kernels pressed
She tempers dulcet creams, nor these to hold
Wants her fit vessels pure, then strews the ground
With rose and odours from the shrub unfumed.
Meanwhile our primitive great sire, to meet
His god-like guest, walks forth, without more train
Accompanied than with his own complete
Perfections; in himself was all his state,
More solemn than the tedious pomp that waits
On princes, when their rich retinue long
Of horses led, and grooms besmeared with gold
Dazzles the crowd, and sets them all agape.
Nearer his presence Adam though not awed,
Yet with submiss approach and reverence meek,
As to a superior nature, bowing low,
    Thus said. Native of Heav'n, for other place
None can than Heav'n such glorious shape contain;
Since by descending from the thrones above,
Those happy places thou hast deigned a while
To want, and honour these, vouchsafe with us

Two only, who yet by sov'reign gift possess
This spacious ground, in yonder shady bow'r
To rest, and what the garden choicest bears
To sit and taste, till this meridian heat
Be over, and the sun more cool decline.
    Whom thus the angelic Virtue answered mild.
Adam, I therefore came, nor art thou such
Created, or such place hast here to dwell,
As may not oft invite, though Spirits of Heav'n
To visit thee; lead on then where thy bow'r
O'ershades; for these mid-hours, till ev'ning rise
I have at will. So to the sylvan lodge
They came, that like Pomona's arbour[2] smiled
With flow'rets decked and fragrant smells; but Eve
Undecked, save with herself more lovely fair
Than wood-nymph, or the fairest goddess feigned
Of three that in Mount Ida naked strove,[3]
Stood to entertain her guest from Heav'n; no veil
She needed, virtue-proof, no thought infirm
Altered her cheek. On whom the angel Hail
Bestowed, the holy salutation used
Long after to blest Mary, second Eve.
    Hail mother of mankind, whose fruitful womb
Shall fill the world more numerous with thy sons
Than with these various fruits the trees of God
Have heaped this table. Raised of grassy turf
Their table was, and mossy seats had round,
And on her ample square from side to side
All autumn piled, though spring and autumn here
Danced hand in hand. A while discourse they hold;
No fear lest dinner cool; when thus began

2. Pomona is the Roman goddess of fruit trees.
3. The three goddesses who strove for the apple on Mount Ida were Juno, Minerva and Venus.

Our author. Heav'nly stranger, please to taste
These bounties which our Nourisher, from whom
All perfect good unmeasured out, descends,
To us for food and for delight hath caused
The earth to yield; unsavoury food perhaps
To spiritual natures; only this I know,
That one celestial Father gives to all.
   To whom the angel. Therefore what he gives
(Whose praise be ever sung) to man in part
Spiritual, may of purest Spirits be found
No ingrateful food: and food alike those pure
Intelligential substances require
As doth your rational; and both contain
Within them every lower faculty
Of sense, whereby they hear, see, smell, touch, taste,
Tasting concoct, digest, assimilate,
And corporeal to incorporeal turn.
For know, whatever was created, needs
To be sustained and fed; of elements
The grosser feeds the purer, earth the sea,
Earth and the sea feed air, the air those fires
Ethereal, and as lowest first the moon;
Whence in her visage round those spots, unpurged
Vapours not yet into her substance turned.
Nor doth the moon no nourishment exhale
From her moist continent to higher orbs.
The sun that light imparts to all, receives
From all his alimental recompense
In humid exhalations, and at even
Sups with the ocean: though in Heav'n the trees
Of life ambrosial fruitage bear, and vines
Yield nectar, though from off the boughs each morn
We brush mellifluous dews, and find the ground
Covered with pearly grain: yet God hath here

Varied his bounty so with new delights,
As may compare with Heaven; and to taste
Think not I shall be nice. So down they sat,
And to their viands fell, nor seemingly
The angel, nor in mist, the common gloss
Of theologians, but with keen dispatch
Of real hunger, and concoctive heat
To transubstantiate; what redounds, transpires
Through Spirits with ease; nor wonder; if by fire
Of sooty coal th' empiric alchemist
Can turn, or holds it possible to turn
Metals of drossiest ore to perfect gold
As from the mine. Meanwhile at table Eve
Ministered naked, and their flowing cups
With pleasant liquors crowned: O innocence
Deserving Paradise! if ever, then,
Then had the sons of God excuse to have been
Enamoured at that sight; but in those hearts
Love unlibidinous reigned, nor jealousy
Was understood, the injured lover's Hell.

Book VII, lines 243–60

God creates light. This is Raphael's description to Adam.

    Let there be light, said God, and forthwith light
Ethereal, first of things, quintessence pure
Sprung from the deep, and from her native east
To journey through the airy gloom began,
Sphered in a radiant cloud, for yet the sun
Was not; she in a cloudy tabernacle
Sojourned the while. God saw the light was good;
And light from darkness by the hemisphere

Divided: light the day, and darkness night
He named. Thus was the first day ev'n and morn:
Nor passed uncelebrated, nor unsung
By the celestial choirs, when orient light
Exhaling first from darkness they beheld;
Birthday of heav'n and earth; with joy and shout
The hollow universal orb they filled,
And touched their golden harps, and hymning praised
God and his works; Creator him they sung,
Both when first ev'ning was, and when first morn.

Book VIII, *lines 588–629*

Raphael and Adam talk of love, Raphael speaking first.
Adam asks an indiscreet question and Raphael, blushing,
reveals that angels enjoy virtual sex.

In loving thou dost well, in passion not,
Wherein true love consists not; love refines
The thoughts, and heart enlarges, hath his seat
In reason, and is judicious, is the scale
By which to Heav'nly love thou may'st ascend,
Not sunk in carnal pleasure, for which cause
Among the beasts no mate for thee was found.
    To whom thus half abashed Adam replied.
Neither her outside formed so fair, nor aught
In procreation common to all kinds
(Though higher of the genial bed by far,
And with mysterious reverence I deem)
So much delights me as those graceful acts,
Those thousand decencies that daily flow
From all her words and actions, mixed with love
And sweet compliance, which declare unfeigned

Union of mind, or in us both one soul;
Harmony to behold in wedded pair
More grateful than harmonious sound to the ear.
Yet these subject not; I to thee disclose
What inward thence I feel, not therefore foiled,
Who meet with various objects, from the sense
Variously representing; yet still free
Approve the best, and follow what I approve.
To love thou blam'st me not, for love thou say'st
Leads up to Heav'n, is both the way and guide;
Bear with me then, if lawful what I ask;
Love not the Heav'nly Spirits, and how their love
Express they, by looks only, or do they mix
Irradiance, virtual or immediate touch?
  To whom the angel with a smile that glowed
Celestial rosy red, love's proper hue,
Answered. Let it suffice thee that thou know'st
Us happy, and without love no happiness.
Whatever pure thou in the body enjoy'st
(And pure thou wert created) we enjoy
In eminence, and obstacle find none
Of membrane, joint, or limb, exclusive bars:
Easier than air with air, if Spirits embrace,
Total they mix, union of pure with pure
Desiring; nor restrained conveyance need
As flesh to mix with flesh, or soul with soul.

Book IX, lines 385–411

Eve decides to go gardening on her own.

... from her husband's hand her hand
Soft she withdrew, and like a wood-nymph light

Oread or Dryad, or of Delia's[1] train,
Betook her to the groves, but Delia's self
In gait surpassed and goddess-like deport,
Though not as she with bow and quiver armed,
But with such gard'ning tools as art yet rude,
Guiltless of fire had formed, or angels brought.
To Pales,[2] or Pomona thus adorned,
Likeliest she seemed, Pomona when she fled
Vertumnus, or to Ceres in her prime,
Yet virgin of Proserpina from Jove.
Her long with ardent look his eye pursued
Delighted, but desiring more her stay.
Oft he to her his charge of quick return
Repeated, she to him as oft engaged
To be returned by noon amid the bow'r,
And all things in best order to invite
Noontide repast, or afternoon's repose.
O much deceived, much failing, hapless Eve,
Of thy presumed return! event perverse!
Thou never from that hour in Paradise
Found'st either sweet repast, or sound repose;
Such ambush hid among sweet flow'rs and shades
Waited with Hellish rancour imminent
To intercept thy way, or send thee back
Despoiled of innocence, of faith, of bliss.

1. Delia is the goddess Diana (born   2. Pales is the goddess of flocks,
on Delos).   Vertumnus a wood god.

Book IX, lines 908–16

Adam, finding that Eve has eaten the forbidden fruit, which they have been told will lead to death, tells her he will eat too and die with her rather than be parted.

How can I live without thee, how forgo
Thy sweet convérse and love so dearly joined,
To live again in these wild woods forlorn?
Should God create another Eve, and I
Another rib afford, yet loss of thee
Would never from my heart; no no, I feel
The link of nature draw me: flesh of flesh,
Bone of my bone thou art, and from thy state
Mine never shall be parted, bliss or woe.

Book X, lines 766–93

Adam soliloquizes about how God intends to punish him and imagines a mother.

God made thee of choice his own, and of his own
To serve him; thy reward was of his grace;
Thy punishment then justly is at his will.
Be it so, for I submit, his doom is fair,
That dust I am, and shall to dust return:
O welcome hour whenever! why delays
His hand to execute what his decree
Fixed on this day? why do I overlive,
Why am I mocked with death, and lengthened out
To deathless pain? how gladly would I meet
Mortality my sentence, and be earth

Insensible, how glad would lay me down
As in my mother's lap! there I should rest
And sleep secure; his dreadful voice no more
Would thunder in my ears, no fear of worse
To me and to my offspring would torment me
With cruel expectation. Yet one doubt
Pursues me still, lest all I cannot die,
Lest that pure breath of life, the spirit of man
Which God inspired, cannot together perish
With this corporeal clod; then in the grave,
Or in some other dismal place, who knows
But I shall die a living death? O thought
Horrid, if true! yet why? it was but breath
Of life that sinned; what dies but what had life
And sin? the body properly hath neither.
All of me then shall die: let this appease
The doubt, since human reach no further knows.

Book XII, lines 610–49

Eve speaks to Adam on waking from sleep, Paradise is
closed to them, and they set out into the world.

  Whence thou return'st, and whither went'st, I know;
For God is also in sleep, and dreams advise,
Which he hath sent propitious, some great good
Presaging, since with sorrow and hearts distress
Wearied I fell asleep: but now lead on;
In me is no delay; with thee to go
Is to stay here; without thee here to stay,
Is to go hence unwilling; thou to me
Art all things under Heav'n, all places thou,
Who for my wilful crime art banished hence.

This further consolation yet secure
I carry hence; though all by me is lost,
Such favour I unworthy am vouchsafed,
By me the promised Seed shall all restore.

   So spake our mother Eve, and Adam heard
Well pleased, but answered not; for now too nigh
Th' Archangel[1] stood, and from the other hill
To their fixed station, all in bright array
The Cherubim descended; on the ground
Gliding metéorous, as ev'ning mist
Ris'n from a river o'er the marish glides,
And gathers ground fast at the labourer's heel
Homeward returning. High in front advanced,
The brandished sword of God before them blazed
Fierce as a comet; which with torrid heat,
And vapour as the Libyan air adust,
Began to parch the temperate clime; whereat
In either hand the hast'ning angel caught
Our ling'ring parents, and to th' eastern gate
Led them direct, and down the cliff as fast
To the subjected plain; then disappeared.
They looking back, all th' eastern side beheld
Of Paradise, so late their happy seat,
Waved over by that flaming brand, the gate
With dreadful faces thronged, and fiery arms:
Some natural tears they dropped, but wiped them soon;
The world was all before them, where to choose
Their place of rest, and Providence their guide;
They hand in hand with wand'ring steps and slow,
Through Eden took their solitary way.

1. Michael.

Lines from Samson Agonistes:
Of that sort of Dramatic Poem which
is called Tragedy

The date of composition is uncertain, and it may have been written over a long period and only finished in the later years. First published in 1671.

'Agonistes' is from the Greek, suggesting a champion or one engaged in a struggle. The story is taken from the Bible, the Old Testament Book of Judges, Chapters 13–16.

Milton resembled Samson in his blindness, in having been let down by a woman he once thought he loved, and in being surrounded by triumphant political enemies.

Lines 1–11

> *Samson.* A little onward lend thy guiding hand
> To these dark steps, a little further on;
> For yonder bank hath choice of sun or shade;
> There I am wont to sit, when any chance
> Relieves me from my task of servile toil,
> Daily in the common prison else enjoined me,
> Where I a prisoner chained, scarce freely draw
> The air imprisoned also, close and damp,
> Unwholesome draught: but here I feel amends,
> The breath of heav'n fresh-blowing pure and sweet,
> With day-spring born; here leave me to respire.

O dark, dark, dark, amid the blaze of noon,
Irrecoverably dark, total eclipse
Without all hope of day!
O first-created beam, and thou great word,
Let there be light, and light was over all;
Why am I thus bereaved thy prime decree?
The sun to me is dark
And silent as the moon,
When she deserts the night
Hid in her vacant interlunar cave.
Since light so necessary is to life,
And almost life itself, if it be true
That light is in the soul,
She all in every part, why was the sight
To such a tender ball as th' eye confined?
So obvious and so easy to be quenched,
And not, as feeling, through all parts diffused,
That she might look at will through every pore?

Lines 667–704

Chorus. God of our fathers, what is man!
That thou towards him with hand so various,
Or might I say contrarious,
Temper'st thy providence through his short course,
Not evenly, as thou rul'st
The angelic orders and inferior creatures mute,
Irrational and brute.
Nor do I name of men the common rout,
That wand'ring loose about

Grow up and perish, as the summer fly,
Heads without name, no more remembered;
But such as thou hast solemnly elected,
With gifts and graces eminently adorned
To some great work, thy glory,
And people's safety, which in part they effect:
Yet toward these thus dignified, thou oft
Amidst their heighth of noon,
Changest thy countenance, and thy hand with no regard
Of highest favours past
From thee on them, or them to thee of service.
   Nor only dost degrade them, or remit
To life obscured, which were a fair dismission,
But throw'st them lower than thou didst exalt them high,
Unseemly falls in human eye,
Too grievous for the trespass or omission;
Oft leav'st them to the hostile sword
Of heathen and profane, their carcasses
To dogs and fowls a prey, or else captíved:
Or to th' unjust tribunals, under change of times,
And condemnation of the ingrateful multitude.
If these they 'scape, perhaps in poverty
With sickness and disease thou bow'st them down,
Painful diseases and deformed,
In crude old age;
Though not disordinate, yet causeless suff'ring
The punishment of dissolute days; in fine,
Just or unjust, alike seem miserable,
For oft alike, both come to evil end.

Nothing is here for tears, nothing to wail
Or knock the breast, no weakness, no contempt,
Dispraise, or blame, nothing but well and fair
And what may quiet us in a death so noble.